instamatic

karma

also by may pang

loving john

photographs of john lennon

by may pang

instamatic karma

k rma

st. martin's press
new york

www.stmartins.com

Design by Kathryn Parise

ISBN-13: 978-0-312-37741-0
ISBN-10: 0-312-37741-X

First Edition: March 2008

10 9 8 7 6 5 4 3 2 1

This book is dedicated to everyone
who loved John.

contents

preface

With a most gracious nod toward the two other major women in John's life—Yoko Ono and Cynthia Lennon—May Pang, loving mother of two, has brought us a rarity—a book full of photographic memory and joy.

Through timing and circumstance, May and John were connected. John was a superstar. May, a loyal employee of John and Yoko's, found herself in a relationship that was superbly deep, meaningful, and yet strangely surreal. While they didn't know what the future held for them, the time May and John spent together and the influence of each on the other was clear and special.

In 1975, John Lennon told me that his time with May was one of the "happiest times of my life." There is no doubt that May Pang feels the same way.

There is also no question that John Lennon's life was filled with extraordinary bursts of raw talent, punctuated with periods of exhilaration and challenge, joy and despair. But as a man who traveled with him, and who wrote about his never-ending search for the truth, I can tell the reader that, as a human being, John always triumphed in the end.

Part of that triumph was due to his amazing curiosity, and the tons of love inside of him; love not only for the people close to him but for all people. John was rich in material terms, but he was richer still as an individual who respected the good in people.

May Pang has captured the curiosity and affection of the real John Lennon in this photographic essay of their time together.

May brings John's life in the mid-seventies back to life. In my career, I've learned that words bring images to the reader. In the case of *Instamatic Karma*, we focus our eyes and our minds on an intimate and private view of an iconic legend who, all along, just wanted to be one of the people.

For those who loved John Lennon and for those who are just discovering him, May Pang's photographic journey is a priceless look at a man who still, years after his death, makes us think, through his music and words, about a better life ahead.

Larry Kane
Author of *Ticket to Ride* and *Lennon Revealed*

introduction

M ost people have come to know the time that John Lennon and I spent together as "The Lost Weekend." I am always surprised at how many people are under the impression that our time together lasted only a single weekend. John and I were together "officially" for eighteen months but our relationship actually spanned ten years—from December 1970 through December 1980.

My association with the Lennons began as a working relationship. For three years, I had a dream job: personal assistant and production coordinator for John and Yoko. A typical day would consist of the mundane (like brewing the morning coffee and opening mail) to calling Jackie Kennedy Onassis or Andy Warhol to coordinating their recording sessions. Each day would hold a surprise.

But the biggest surprise of all came in the summer of 1973, as I was coordinating press for Yoko's new album, *Feeling the Space*—and simultaneously starting the sessions for John's upcoming album, *Mind Games*. Early one morning, Yoko came to my office in their apartment at the Dakota and told me that she and John were "not getting along." It was obvious to all of us who worked there that things were a bit tense between them, so this wasn't exactly a bombshell. Yoko went on to say that John would start seeing someone new, and she wanted it to be "someone who would treat John well." I now felt the bombshell coming. I was thinking, *If they split, who will I be working for?*

Yoko continued, *"You* don't have a boyfriend." I dropped my pad and pen. Did I just hear right? I assured her I wasn't interested in John, if that's what she was thinking. She told me she knew that. But she didn't stop there. "I think *you* should go out with him."

I was dumbfounded. I kept telling her no, I would not go out with John. But apparently her mind was made up. "If John asks you out, you should go!" Yoko announced, making it sound a little stronger than a suggestion.

For the next two weeks, all was quiet. Recording was put on hold, and I assumed (and hoped) that John and Yoko had worked out their differences and everything was back to normal. When John resumed recording *Mind Games,* I got ready to accompany him to the studio, as usual. The moment we got into the elevator at the Dakota, my world changed. John grabbed me and kissed me and said, "I've been waiting to do that all fuckin' day."

As we drove to the studio, I sat there speechless while John kept assuring me that "it's O.K., don't be frightened, everything will be alright."

After the session, John told me that he was coming home with me. I just couldn't deal with it, so I ordered the car to take him to the Dakota. After a couple of nights of trying to come home with me and getting rebuffed, he sent the car away during a session without my knowing it.

"We're getting a cab and I'm coming home with you," he declared. I wasn't going to argue on the streets of New York at 2:00 A.M. And so our relationship began.

Shortly after *Mind Games* was completed, Yoko flew to Chicago for a three-day feminist seminar. John's lawyer, Harold Seider, was about to leave for Los Angeles. At the spur of the moment, John thought it would be good for us to leave New York and be on our own, so we headed to L.A. with Harold, much to Harold's surprise.

I hardly had time to pack and tell my mother. I threw a few things together and I grabbed my Nikkormat 35mm camera. John later bought me a new Polaroid SX-70 for my birthday (as well as a used 1968 Barracuda, which was my *very cool* first car).

In L.A., we saw old friends and made new ones. We also began taking road trips because John wanted to experience America. He encouraged me to capture our times together. Photography had always been a bit of a hobby for me so this was natural. He "really liked my eye for taking pictures" and felt I captured him in ways that no one else had because of his comfort level with me. Needless to say, I was very flattered.

In those days, nobody thought of taking photos all the time. We always thought there'd be tomorrow. Many of what are now considered historic events, like John and Paul's only jam session after The Beatles, weren't photographed. I'm surprised I actually captured as many moments as I did.

Of course there were times I was a bit reticent in taking out my camera, particularly when "old friends" stopped by just to hang out. I didn't want to intrude on these moments, but John insisted.

For years, only my closest friends got to see most of these photos—which were literally tucked away in a shoe box in my closet. They were surprised that these images did not convey the John who was portrayed in the press during our time together. In fact, the photos showed a side of John seldom seen.

Every photograph in this book holds a very special memory for me—especially the ones I took of John with his then ten-year-old son, Julian. When John laid eyes on him for the first time in four years, he was shocked to see "a little man" and not the small child he remembered. They spent a lot of time getting reacquainted as father and son, playing guitar and making music together. They were both good swimmers (which I was not, enabling me to capture some rare moments of togetherness).

As I started going through my shoe box of photos, the memories of our happy—and sometimes zany—time together came back, opening up a floodgate of emotions, from happiness to sadness and back to happiness. When I look back on some of the lovable loonies who shared this time with us, everyone seems so young, so vibrant. So many have left us too soon. In my life, I've loved them all.

The best part is that I feel these images bring John back to life. In this book I share with you John Lennon...through my eyes.

May Pang
New York City
October 2007

at home

california, here
we come

Shortly after John and I got together, he decided we would go to Los Angeles for a while. We hopped on a flight with "Uncle" Harold Seider, John's lawyer and trusted advisor from the Allen Klein/ABKCO days (John had hired Harold after he left ABKCO, which came in handy in John's lawsuit against Klein). Harold graciously offered us his apartment and found somewhere else to stay. He knew better than anyone that John had no spending money! We soon met up with two of John's old friends: Rolling Stone Bill Wyman and the Stones' ex-manager, Andrew Loog Oldham. Hanging out with Andrew was always good fun. He was staying at legendary producer Lou Adler's house in Bel Air (Lou had another place in Malibu). Since Andrew would only be in L.A. a few more days, he suggested we ask Lou if we could use the place. We'd put Harold out long enough, so we thought it was a good idea. We didn't know Lou, so Andrew arranged it for us. We ended up staying there close to two months. These pictures, taken poolside at Adler's house, are the first I took of our time together.

the beach house

lthough some people are under the impression that John and I spent our entire year and a half together in Los Angeles, we actually only spent about six months living and working there (from September 1973 to early May 1974—with many long breaks back in New York throughout).

During this time, we certainly generated a lot more press than we cared to. From the notorious Phil Spector sessions at A&M (where liquor was poured down a mixing console) and Record Plant West Studios (the scene of the now infamous Spector gun incident), to the two Troubadour incidents: when John wore a Kotex on his forehead and, two months later, when he was "shown the door" for drunkenly heckling the Smothers Brothers (at the exuberant instigation of Harry Nilsson). As John put it, "We had some moments, folks!"

While in L.A., we sometimes stayed at the Beverly Wilshire Hotel or at the homes of friends, but the most infamous place we called home was a rented Santa Monica beach house.

The beach house had quite an illustrious past. It was built by film producer Louis B. Mayer, was quite "Hollywood" in design, and was a hot spot for movie business royalty back in the day. It was later owned by actor Peter Lawford, who continued the tradition by hosting fellow Hollywood luminaries as well as his brothers-in-law, President John F. Kennedy and Attorney General Robert F. Kennedy, on many occasions. Allegedly, Marilyn Monroe had been a frequent visitor—which greatly piqued John's interest.

When John decided to produce Harry Nilsson's *Pussy Cats* album, he thought it would be a great idea to have everyone who was working on it living under one roof. This way, they could discuss and rehearse the tracks, and—most important—everyone would get to the studio on time. John was a stickler for promptness and professionalism when working. It seemed like a good idea...until you considered the cast of characters.

The house came equipped with Armando and Maria Ontivero, a great couple who were the caretakers (and who became *our* caretakers). They fed and looked after us every day. John and I took the master bedroom. When we first saw it, he said, "So, this is where they did it," referring to the former presidential guest and Monroe. The other five bedrooms were occupied by Keith Moon, Harry, Hilary Gerrard (Ringo's business manager), and Klaus Voormann. To our immediate left, complete with an official portrait of President Kennedy on the wall, was a library, which was converted to a bedroom for Ringo.

Although we could still see remnants of the home's historic splendor, the new owners obviously didn't feel the need to preserve the original decor. They had sealed up the huge projection screen installed by Mayer and they covered the expensive parquet floors with a hideous 70's shag carpet. We did discover a doorway to a small poker room that remained untouched, and became a popular room with us.

Among our regular visitors were drummer Jim Keltner, guitarist Jesse Ed Davis, ex-Beatle roadie Mal Evans, Peter "Dougal" Butler (Keith Moon's assistant), and Paul and Linda McCartney with their girls. It seemed that everyone in town popped up there at least once during our stay.

There's that shag carpet.

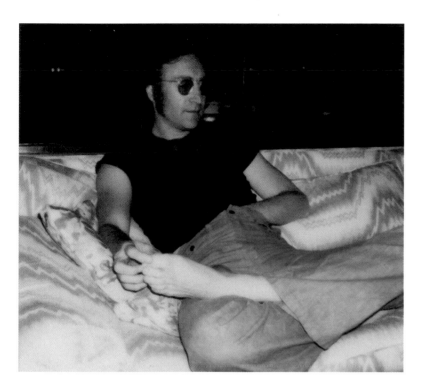

The 70s were
about rainbows
and toe socks.

14

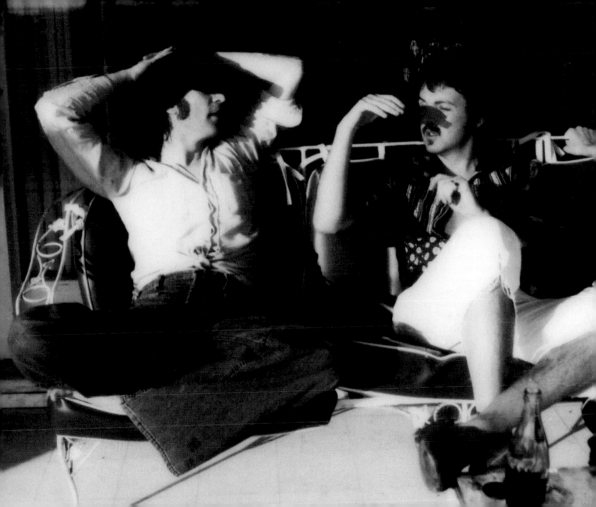

"Baron Von Moon" as he would greet us each day—in his long leather coat, scarf, boots, and with briefcase in hand, but no trousers! Every morning Moon made a point of making sure everyone knew he was awake....John always acknowledged him with "Morning, Baron."

Poolside at the
beach house: John,
Mal Evans (back),
and Ringo.

our apartment,
new york city

We decided to find a permanent home in New York in May 1974. My cramped studio on East 89th was fine for a pit stop, but it wasn't going to work for the long term. While John was working on *Pussy Cats*, Eddie Germano, general manager of Record Plant Studios, told us there was an apartment available in his building.

The address was 434 East 52nd Street. The apartment we looked at was called the Ponthouse Tower B. When we opened the front door, we were greeted by a steep staircase that led up to a rooftop apartment. Although it was a small one-bedroom, it had a nice kitchen, a large living room with a working fireplace, and a balcony that overlooked the East River (which is where we would see the UFO that John referred to in the booklet for *Walls and Bridges*). We ended up using the living room as our bedroom and entertaining center, and kept the small bedroom as a dressing room and as Julian's room when he came to stay.

One great advantage of living in that apartment building was having a neighbor like Eddie. He was the guy to go to if you needed anything, and he would always oblige John. If John needed anything at the studio, he'd tell Eddie and it'd be ready when we got there. He even outfitted our apartment with a state-of-the-art sound system so John would be enveloped in sound and could study his mixes.

We brought in a platform king-size bed and the largest-screen TV available in those days: a twenty-seven-inch Sony Trinitron. Our bed became "Lennon Central"—with the cable box, telephone, and sound system all within reach. John dreamed his hit song "#9 Dream" in this bed.

Someone's knockin at the door . . .
(by the way, the street sign above the door was
something I grabbed when the city was changing
from the porcelain signs to aluminum)

Linda and Paul McCartney

Mick Jagger and Bebe Buell

David Bowie and Ava Cherry

POSITION A:
Lying in bed,
watching the
telly, reading
the papers.

One day while John was recording, the studio receptionist brought in a litter of kittens. John immediately knew what I was thinking and said, "No, we can't, we're traveling too much."

I picked up a black one and put him over my shoulder. When I came back into the recording room with him, John rolled his eyes and said, "Now you've done it! Now you've done it!" I had a moment of wondering what I'd done, when he came over, started petting him, and said, "Well I guess we have to have a cat."

At the end of the day when we were leaving the studio, John asked if there were any left. We went back to get the only kitten that remained—a white one that no one wanted because she was so loud. John christened them Major and Minor. He loved those cats. They reminded him of his days with Aunt Mimi (whom he playfully referred to as the "Cat Woman").

Like father, like son.

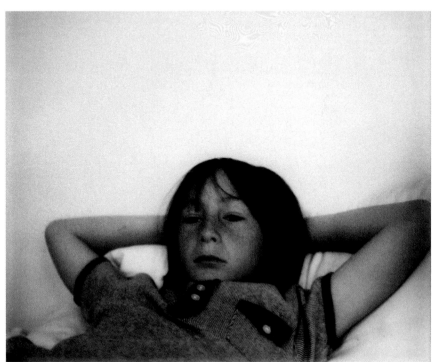

This fiery halo appeared over Julian's head as the Polaroid developed, which prompted John to quip, "My boy's pretty hot stuff."

Julian goes "incognito" in his dad's clothing.

The multitalented
Julian was our
photographer for
these two shots.

31

soup's on!

John had a voracious appetite, which comes as a surprise to many people. We had a tradition every Sunday: At 11:00 A.M. I'd come in with *The New York Times,* some of the British papers, and coffee (he gave up tea in America because it was decidedly British. He'd say, "When in Rome . . ."). I would make a big English breakfast of bacon and eggs, beans on toast with tomatoes, chips, and sometimes black pudding, after I discovered a local Irish butcher who carried it. (Cynthia Lennon once tried to smuggle some in for us, but it was confiscated.) John was over the moon about it. I didn't know how to cook it at first, so I asked John, who said, "Just fry it up." Those sausages really stunk up the kitchen, but he loved them.

John also loved Chinese food—especially my mom's. When we were home in New York, she would always bring us her specialty: fried rice and spare ribs. As unconventional as John was, he was also old-fashioned. Because of the nature of our relationship, John felt uneasy about meeting my mom. He never did meet her, which he later regretted. He would literally hide behind the door until she left. Of course, he had no problem inhaling the food she brought. Here he is enjoying his favorite hot & sour soup.

The soup is doing its job.

As he's blowing his nose, John jokes, "Is nothing sacred?"

at play

long island sound

One day, Eddie asked John if he was into sailing. Boy, did he ask the right person. The sea was in John's blood. Not only was he born in the major port city of Liverpool but his father was a merchant seaman. Not one for pools, he preferred an open body of salt water. He would swim every day if he could. At the sea, he found peace of mind and recharged his creativity.

Eddie and his wife, Janice, had a thirty-seven-foot boat moored on Long Island Sound at New Rochelle, New York. The Sound is an inlet of the Atlantic Ocean bordered by New York, Connecticut, and, of course, Long Island. It soon became one of our favorite things to do—jump in the car with the Germanos and head up to the Sound with their two children, Danielle and Troy. When Julian came to visit, we took him, and they'd all have a great time swimming and playing together in the water.

On this particular outing, John was trying to teach me how to swim, but he couldn't get me to let go of the boat, much less into the water. It wasn't happening. I kept seeing the headline: JOHN LENNON DROWNS TEACHING GIRLFRIEND TO SWIM. Instead, I went back onto the boat and grabbed my camera and caught John at his most serene.

He once mentioned that a photo of him floating weightlessly on the water would make a good album cover.

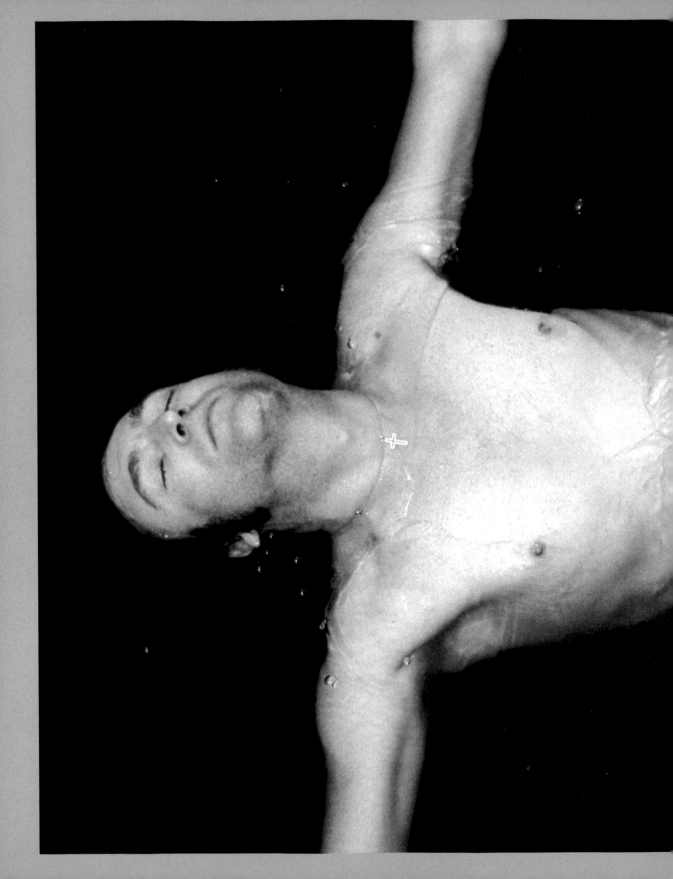

central park

In early November 1974, *Walls and Bridges* and "Whatever Gets You Thru the Night" were rocketing to the top of the charts. In now-legendary radio interviews to promote the album, John displayed a confidence, approachability, humbleness, and renewed sense of humor that sounded like the John of old. This was definitely a happy time for him; for us.

John had made peace with Paul and was starting to feel very sentimental toward The Beatles...just as Robert Stigwood was in production on an off-Broadway play at the Beacon Theatre called *Sgt. Pepper's Lonely Hearts Club Band on the Road*. John was more than happy to help "Stiggy" promote it. He attended rehearsals, offered production suggestions, and did his best to talk up the show. In fact, John even agreed to roam the streets of New York City for a BBC film shoot to plug it.

At some point, a college student asked if he could tag along and film John for his final project. John was in a really good mood that day and agreed. The kid managed to film most of John's day frolicking through the streets of Manhattan. Locales included Central Park, Tiffany's on Fifth Avenue, and the seedy peep shows of Times Square. Not one to waste an opportunity, John also shot a video for "Whatever Gets You Thru the Night" the same day.

We spent a lot of time filming in the park. John fed the elephants at the zoo, did some "magic tricks" for astonished fans (he commandeered a hot dog cart and seemingly made soda and pretzels disappear). He also burst into a cinema verité performance of "John performing for John" at the Central Park Bandshell. It was here, while he was dancing around, jumping for joy, and roundly applauding himself, that I finally got to sit down and take some snapshots.

To me, these photos sum up John's love of life and love for New York.

at work

king as "queen"

When we first arrived in Los Angeles, John began promoting his soon-to-be-released *Mind Games* album. His previous album, *Some Time in New York City*, had been universally panned by the critics and sold poorly. John was hurt by the rejection of his music, so he was taking this new album very seriously.

Tony King, general manager of Apple Records U.K., happened to be vacationing in L.A. and soon became one of our closest friends. Ever the professional, he offered some sage career advice.

Tony gingerly explained to John that the world now perceived him as an angry radical, which wouldn't bode well for record sales. He needed to get back to being the jovial, witty guy everyone loved. Tony lined up a slew of prominent interviews and John, taking Tony's advice, was definitely back on track.

One night, John and I were hanging out with Tony and his friend, songwriter Michael Hazelwood (with whom Tony was staying). Over a bottle of wine and many laughs, more talk of promoting *Mind Games* came up. As the evening progressed, Tony began an impromptu imitation of the Queen of England, which was so dead-on it had us in hysterics. John even took out a cassette recorder to keep the impression for posterity. Somehow the idea was hatched that Her Royal Majesty herself should promote *Mind Games*.

Well, She wasn't available, so Tony stepped in and gave the royal performance for the television and radio spots. The commercial was shot on October 24, 1973 (my twenty-third birthday). Also attending the shoot was Record Plant East studio owner and chief engineer Roy Cicala and his new assistant, Jimmy Iovine, Elton John (who also took some photos), and Elliot Mintz (a press representative and DJ who had interviewed and befriended Yoko in 1971).

The official press photo for the *Mind Games* LP.

We used this outtake photo from the commercial shoot as our Christmas card in 1974.

On the same day, John bought me my first car—a used reddish 1968 Barracuda—for my birthday. He was tired of having others drive us around, especially because they'd often come late—or not at all. "We're cutting out the middle man," he said as he handed me the keys.

pussy cats

After *Mind Games* was completed, John was energized and raring to go—but he wanted to try some new things musically. First and foremost, he wanted to record an album of his favorite rock 'n' roll songs, the classics he loved as a kid which inspired him to form a band in the first place, such as "Ain't That a Shame," the first song John's mom taught him to play, and "Be-Bop-A-Lula," the song John was playing on stage with the Quarrymen the day he met Paul McCartney. Second, he wanted to produce an album for someone else. This would give John a chance to be more creative with sound and not get caught up with being "John Lennon."

John had begun his "Oldies" album with Phil Spector at the helm, but the notorious sessions fueled by alcohol had gotten so out of hand that John decided to temporarily shelve the project. But he was still keen on producing another artist.

John knew Harry from back in England, and once pronounced Harry his "favorite American group," but they really hit it off again when Ringo reintroduced them. John thought he had the most beautiful voice, and since they were hanging out and getting into all kinds of mischief, John figured, why not do something productive.

Thus *Pussy Cats* was born. The album was an eclectic mix of songs: some written by Harry, some classic oldies mostly chosen by John, a couple of contemporary favorites, and a Lennon composition combined with a Jamaican traditional song, "Mucho Mungo/Mt. Elga."

Recording began at Burbank Studios on March 28, 1974. (Later that same evening, to everyone's surprise, Paul and Linda dropped in for a visit. That night John and Paul ended up playing together for the one and only time since The Beatles. Stevie Wonder also came by unannounced and joined in on the impromptu jam.) As I did for John's albums, I served as production coordinator. This album proved a bit of a challenge at times, what with three drummers: Ringo, Jim Keltner, and Keith Moon (four if you count John taking a stab at it)—

and having to schedule around Harry's on-again, off-again voice, which was suffering the ravages of heavy drinking. There must've been something in the California air—between the *Pussy Cats* sessions and John's initial *Rock 'n' Roll* sessions, the studio mood was a bit more "party" than John was accustomed to. Things were not going as John had planned.

Ultimately, John moved the final production of *Pussy Cats* to New York, where the work ethic was decidedly more professional—and where he thought he could control Harry. He completed the album in the familiar environment of Record Plant East.

As was his habit, John always did something really nice for people before he said good-bye. Armed with the completed album in hand, Harry, John, and I marched into Ken Glancy's office at RCA Records in New York, where John enthusiastically talked up Harry's artistry. He even coyly suggested that he and Ringo might join RCA when their Apple contracts were up, but would have no interest in doing so unless Harry was with the label. As Harry sat there quietly, John secured him the most lucrative recording deal of his career. Afterwards, we went out to celebrate. This turned out to be the last time we saw Harry while John and I were together.

These are some photos from the *Pussy Cats* sessions at Burbank Studios.

A rare shot of John on drums.

Listening to a playback.

John scarfing down some sparc ribs during the recording session. He wasn't very discriminating—pizza, Chinese, pancakes, he loved it all. I had to ship cases of Dr Pepper over to England to fuel the *Imagine* sessions, while *Walls and Bridges* and *Rock 'n' Roll* were recorded on Burger King Whoppers, deli sandwiches, and Coca-Cola.

walls and bridges,
june 1974

fter *Pussy Cats* was completed, John wanted to get back to his own music. He thought about resuming the "Oldies" album, but Phil Spector, who supposedly had had a serious motorcycle accident, was incommunicado, and held the session tapes hostage. So John, with a stockpile of new songs, plunged into a fresh original album, *Walls and Bridges*.

Capitol Records was expecting the "Oldies" album next, and the cover for that was already in production. It would feature drawings John had made as a child. John thought that the cover could also suit this album, but when Capitol learned John would deliver an album of original material, they decided on a more lavish design.

They would still use the drawings, but asked John for a series of photos—close-ups of his face with different expressions. John asked me to take them. I did a series of test shots, which John loved. However, because of the unique cover design, the art director needed the images in a two-inch format from a Hasselblad, which I did not have. John eventually gave his O.K. to let Bob Gruen take the photos on our East 52nd Street balcony. This is the same day that John posed for the famous shot where he's wearing a New York City T-shirt, also on our balcony. While Bob took his photos, I captured some of the session behind the scenes.

Following pages: A few of my original test shots for the
Walls and Bridges cover, taken on the roof of Record Plant
Studios East, on the day he recorded "Surprise, Surprise
(Sweet Bird of Paradox)," the song John wrote for me.

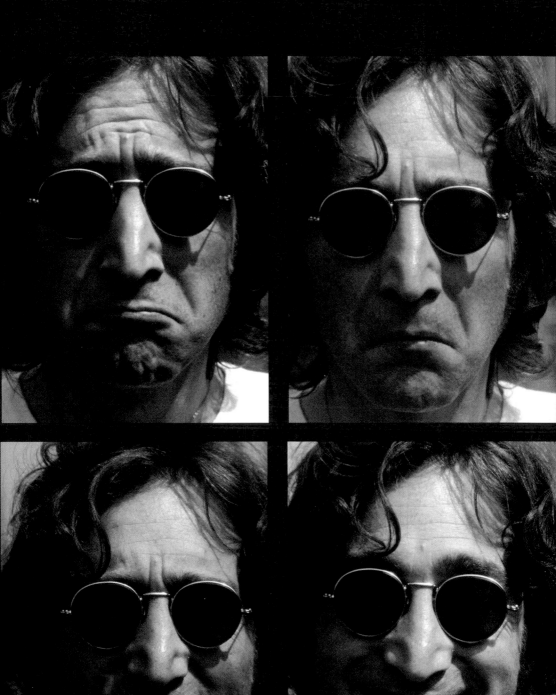

Every song on *Walls and Bridges* has a distinctive production and instrumental lineup.
John wrote one of the first songs for it, "Nobody Loves You (When You're Down And Out),"
at Lou Adler's. It was inspired by a trip we took to Las Vegas. John actually wrote it for
Frank Sinatra, complete with the schmaltzy horns and "show biz" lyrics. He envisioned it as
a big closing number for Frank in Vegas.

Here's John with Kenny Ascher on our balcony discussing John's orchestral arrange-
ments while looking out onto the East River. When Kenny wrote out the charts, he had
added a couple of notes to a string line John created. John immediately noticed, which
took Kenny by surprise. Kenny didn't realize how focused and meticulous John was with
every nuance of each song. I also took a few shots of John conducting "Little Big Horns."

John clowning with
Jim Keltner.

Arthur Jenkins, percussionist
extraordinaire. He'd light up,
sit in the corner, and do his
thing. John thought he was
amazing and used him on
practically every album.

The Three Musketeers: Jimmy Iovine, John, and Bobby Keys taking a break on the roof of Record Plant East while recording "Beef Jerky."

listen to this . . .

T he year 1974 marked the tenth anniversary of The Beatles conquering America. Capitol Records celebrated by embarking on a full-scale promotional campaign to reintroduce the band, and then along comes John with a new album. Timing is everything. Capitol loved John's new album and agreed to a full marketing blitz. They were pleased that John would be very actively involved, working closely with Al Coury and Bruce Wendell, Capitol's senior vice president of promotion. It was John who coined the "Listen To This…" slogan.

In a nutshell, the campaign consisted of LISTEN TO THIS (whatever the item was), a picture of John's eyes and nose, and JOHN LENNON WALLS AND BRIDGES at the bottom. The items included: a LISTEN TO THIS poster, ad, postcard, cash register, button, photo, press kit, matchbook, envelope, bus (on New York City buses), songbook, mobile, dream (a special ad for the second single, "#9 Dream") and a long-sleeved T-shirt (which John designed–I still have his sketches). There was a LISTEN TO THIS television commercial, which Ringo did (John returned the favor and did the commercial for Ringo's *Goodnight Vienna* album).

When John and I went to L.A. to promote the album, I snapped a photo of a huge LISTEN TO THIS billboard atop Tower Records on Sunset Blvd. We then went inside, where there was an elaborate custom display for the album. Fans lucky enough to be buying it when we walked in got autographed copies.

king of america

John encouraged Tony King to relocate to the United States. "It's better to work for us here, where all the action is," said John. Soon Tony was set up with a dinky windowless office at Capitol Records. Taking a page from Tony's P.R. book, John orchestrated a "big announcement" to introduce Tony to America, and he insisted I take the press photos. Since Ringo was in town, we roped him in for the photos as well. After we saw Tony's horrible office, John and Ringo personally wrote to Bhaskar Menon, chairman and CEO of EMI/Capitol, and asked him to improve Tony's accommodations, which was done promptly.

No, it's not Sonny Bono…This is Al Coury, vice-president and head of promotion and A&R for Capitol Records. Al was a genius at knowing which songs would be smash hits. He had worked wonders on Paul's *Band On The Run* album, so John was pleased to be working with him. John had no clue as to what the single from *Walls and Bridges* should be. John convened a meeting of his "kitchen cabinet," which consisted of me, Tony King, and Al and we went back and forth about all the possible selections. Of course, "#9 Dream" was a strong contender, as was "Surprise, Surprise" and even "Move Over Ms. L" (which was cut from the album at the last minute). Al chose "Whatever Gets You Thru the Night," which John wasn't too sure about—so much so that he bet Elton John that it wouldn't hit #1. Fortunately for us, he lost that bet and, to make good, performed with Elton at Madison Square Garden, Thanksgiving, November 28, 1974, which turned out to be his last major public performance.

The day this photo was taken, John and the band were just starting the rehearsals for *Walls and Bridges* when Al burst into Record Plant East saying, "I got them! I got the tapes!" referring to the oldies tapes from the Spector sessions. John was in no mood to deal with them in the middle of making an original album, so he put them in the vault until the new record was completed.

morris levy had
a farm . . .

Morris Levy was one of the most colorful characters in the music industry, widely known as the "Godfather of American Rock 'n' Roll"—a name not bestowed because of his paternal instincts.

John's history with Morris dated back to 1969, when John wrote "Come Together," a kind of homage to his hero, Chuck Berry. Apparently, Morris thought it a bit too close to its inspiration, Berry's "You Can't Catch Me."

Morris, who owned and published the tune, sued John for plagiarism. Just as the case was about to go to trial in 1973, the Spector sessions began. John didn't want to interrupt the recording, so he instructed his lawyers to make a settlement to avoid his having to fly to New York. John agreed to record three Levy-published songs on the upcoming oldies album.

Things didn't quite work out that way. John's next album turned out to be *Walls and Bridges,* but he did include a snippet of the Levy catalogue's "Ya-Ya," with Julian accompanying his dad on the drums, tagged onto the end. At the beginning of the song, John says, "Let's do sitting in the La-La and get rid of that!"—a little joke aimed at Morris, who failed to see the humor. He voiced his displeasure to John, and John assured him that the next album would be the oldies and he'd honor his commitment.

But John was growing frustrated with the album, now entering its second year of non-completion. "This is getting grotesque," he moaned. "All I wanted to do was record a simple, straightforward rock 'n' roll album—I didn't even want to play, just sing—and it's become more time-consuming and complicated than *Sgt. Pepper*. Hell, when I started this thing, it was a novel idea. Now the oldies crest has come and gone. Everyone's done the oldies. It's become old hat."

In fact, John even toyed with calling the album *Old Hat*.

Morris became a close friend of ours at this point, monitoring the progress of what would eventually become the *Rock 'n' Roll* album. When John said he would use the band from *Walls and Bridges* to complete *Rock 'n' Roll,* Morris graciously offered us the use of his farm upstate in Ghent, New York, to rehearse the tracks.

A few limos drove us and the minimal equipment up to the farm. As we got closer, John would ask as we passed each typical wooden farmhouse, "Is that it?" and Morris would chuckle. When we finally arrived at the huge compound and saw the mansion Morris lived in, John said, "In which wing do the cows sleep?"

The décor was a little ornate—marble floors, glistening Italian tile, gold-plated faucets in the bathroom where the water flowed from fish-head spouts. John described it as "Early American brothel."

The leader of
the band.

(Clockwise) The late Jesse Ed Davis, Klaus Voormann, Eddie Mottau, and Kenny Ascher rehearsing *Rock 'n' Roll* at the farm.

the dream is over

After three years of court battles, public and private acrimony, and millions of dollars, the final dissolution of The Beatles was about to happen. With just a few more kinks left to iron out, the dissolution meeting was set to take place at The Plaza hotel in New York City—ironically, the first place the group stayed in America in 1964 (and just a short walk from our apartment).

It was scheduled for December 19, 1974, when George would be in New York on his *Dark Horse* tour. Paul and Linda came in, and of course John and I were already here. Julian was with us for the Christmas holidays, and for the moment, all was calm, all was bright. John was even planning to join George on stage at Madison Square Garden.

At The Plaza, George, with his lawyer, David Braun, and business manager, Denis O'Brien; the McCartneys, with Paul's in-laws and lawyers, Lee and John Eastman; Ringo's lawyer, Bruce Grakal, and business manager, Hilary Gerrard; and Neil Aspinall, with two teams of lawyers for Apple (one for the U.S. and one for the U.K.) gathered around a very large table to get all the signatures on the paperwork dissolving the partnership. Ringo wasn't there because he was ducking a subpoena from Allen Klein, but he had already signed the documents back in England. They had him on long distance to confirm he was "alive." John's lawyer and advisor, Harold Seider, was there along with his team, David Dolgenos and Michael Graham. Paul and Linda had a camera set up to document the historic occasion.

Harold told me that after a while, George said out loud what everyone was thinking: "Well, where's John?"

"Good question," replied Harold, who was wondering himself.

Harold left the room to call John, who wouldn't get on the phone. I was home with John. It was up to me to tell Harold that John had decided not to go to the meeting at The Plaza. Although John was concerned with shouldering a major tax burden because he lived in the United States, I could sense there was a little bit more on his mind. His official reason for not showing was "the stars aren't right."

George, already in a dour mood because his tour was getting poor reviews and his voice was shot, went ballistic. He started yelling at Harold and blamed him for John not coming. Soon, all the other lawyers erupted at Harold. George then picked up the phone and called John, but got me. I asked if he wanted John, and he barked, "No! Just tell him whatever his problem is, I started this tour on my own and I'll end it on my own!" and slammed the phone down. John was listening over my shoulder. Paul and Linda came by the next day, realizing John was upset with the proposed deal. Paul assured John "we'll work it all out."

George's rage didn't last long. When Julian went to George's concert the next day, Neil Aspinall, John, and I went to talk with Lee Eastman, Linda's father. While there, Julian called with a message from George: "All's forgiven, George loves you and he wants you to come to his party tonight." We did go the party at the Hippopotamus Club, where George, John, and Paul hugged. John, Julian, and I left New York the following day to spend Christmas in West Palm Beach, Florida.

On December 29, 1974, the voluminous documents were brought down to John in Florida by one of Apple's lawyers. "Take out your camera, Linda," he joked to me. Then he called Harold Seider to go over some final points.

When John hung up the phone, he looked wistfully out the window. I could almost see him replaying the entire Beatles experience in his mind.

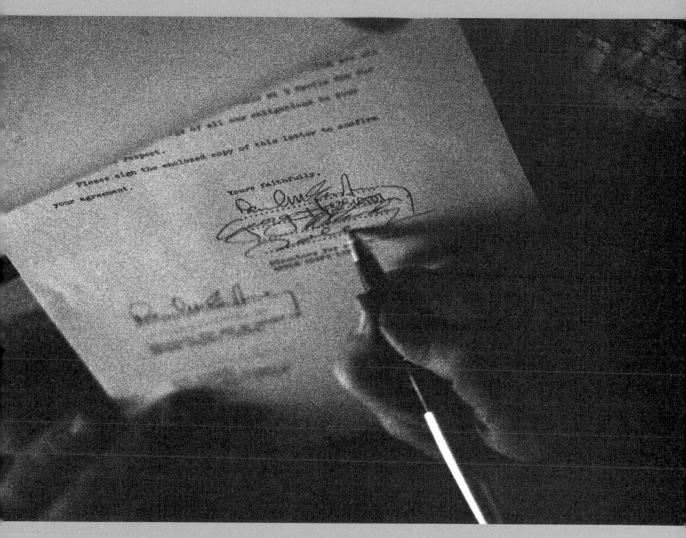

He finally picked up his pen and, in the unlikely backdrop of Disney World, at the Polynesian Village Hotel, officially ended the greatest rock 'n' roll band in history by simply scrawling *John Lennon* at the bottom of the page.

away

ghost town

I n early October 1973, John and I went to Las Vegas for a few days on a lark. We flew there from Los Angeles on a shuttle booked by Elliot Mintz, who came along with us. When we boarded the plane, we found our seats were in the middle of the aircraft. Everybody was going nuts over John, who looked over at Elliot and said, "Why are we back here in the middle of all this?" When Elliot explained it was a shuttle and there was no first-class seating, John snapped, "Please think before putting me in this situation again!" all the while cordially signing autographs and greeting fellow passengers.

When we landed we went straight to Caesar's Palace and did all the touristy stuff. We made a beeline to the casino and even had our photos taken by the house photographer while we were eating. We also arranged to meet up with Tony King and Michael Hazelwood, who drove up from L.A. We saw that one of John's idols, Fats Domino, was playing at the Flamingo (with Frankie Valli as the opening act) so we all went down to catch the show.

Elliot left after a couple of days, so John and I spent the rest of the time hanging out with Tony and Michael. When we'd had enough of Vegas, we piled into Tony's green Thunderbird and drove back to L.A. On the way, we happened upon a ghost town called Calico, an old mining town that had become a tourist attraction. It was a great pit stop for us, just wandering around in the middle of the desert. Calico was a real slice of Americana, right out of a history book or western movie.

One morning John woke me up by saying, "Look, I'm wearing your jeans!"

"So I see," I said. "Why?"

"Because they fit. I love them!"

He never gave them back. When I
realized they had now become *his*, I
thought it wise to remove the butter-
flies and flowers I had embroidered on
them (remember, this was the 70s). In
this picture, you can still see my
needlework.

Tony, John, and
Michael in Calico.

John and Tony.

John and the late Michael Hazelwood. In collaboration with Albert Hammond, Michael wrote some classic songs including "It Never Rains in Southern California," "Gimme Dat Ding," and The Hollies' smash hit, "The Air That I Breathe." He also played acoustic guitar on the *Rock 'n' Roll* album, which he was very excited about.

(Next page) As we wandered around, John noticed this Harley Trike motorcycle. He kept eying it, so I finally said, "Just go over to it and I'll take a picture." I only took this single shot, which fortunately came out pretty good. After I took this photo, John joked in a Bogey-esque drawl, "Hop on, kid, let's blow this joint."

These are the
photos of John
and me taken
at dinner in
Caesars Palace,
still in the orig-
inal holder.

John and me stepping
out on the town, Los
Angeles, 1974.

And here we are at one of the
many parties we attended in
the Hollywood Hills. On any
given night, we'd run into the
usual suspects like Harry,
Ringo, Micky Dolenz, Jack
Nicholson, Warren Beatty,
Roman Polanski, Cher, Jimmy
Webb, Danny Hutton (Three
Dog Night), Cheech and
Chong, or the Beach Boys
(including Brian Wilson).

christmas at disneyland, 1973

T his was the first of Julian's many visits with his dad while John and I were together. John hadn't seen his son in almost four years and it was nerve-racking for
John to figure out how to communicate with him. He also hadn't seen Cynthia
since their painful divorce, and since she was bringing Julian, that also was cause for great
angst. When they arrived, we met them at the airport in a stretch limo and brought them
to the Beverly Hills Hotel, first-class treatment all the way.

After the initial awkwardness subsided, it was up to me to become the "tour director"
for Julian's visit. Of course, the biggest attraction there for any ten-year-old kid is
Disneyland. So off we went with Jesse Ed Davis, his girlfriend, Patti, and her son, who was
roughly the same age as Julian. Mal Evans, who was still working for the individual guys,
drove us all down. It was also good for Mal to see Julian again, and the 6' 4" teddy bear
ended up on the teacup ride with Julian.

John with Jesse Ed Davis in the background.

Mal Evans was one of John's oldest and most trusted friends. When he was killed in early January 1976, John took it very badly. As he always had a hard time dealing with the loss of people in his life, John's humor was his defense mechanism. When he learned that Mal's ashes were lost en route to England, John suggested, "Perhaps they should check the dead letter office."

palm springs, march 1974

Before starting work on *Pussy Cats*, John wanted to clear his head of the Spector sessions. He had also just come off a month of notable publicity—the two Troubadour incidents and the public "outing" of us as a couple. (*Time* magazine had a photographer who was tracking us. John planted a big kiss on my mouth and said, "The secret's out." The photo ran in the issue.) So we thought it would be a great idea if we all went on a little holiday, and since Harry had a doctor's appointment in Palm Springs, that's where we decided to go for a long weekend. Harry brought along his friend, fellow RCA recording artist Sarah Kernochan (who went on to win a couple of Oscars for documentaries she produced), and Mal Evans drove us down.

Things got off to an iffy start when Mal was stopped for speeding. A highway cop pulled us over, but Mal got out of it by saying, "I'm, err, driving (motioning with his head toward John) to a very important..." and the cop took one look at John and went into shock. Mal kept talking, babbling nonsense, knowing the cop wasn't listening at all. He just let us go.

The first night there, Harry said he knew of a great restaurant on top of a mountain. It was only accessible by aerial tram, so off we went. Harry and John had a few drinks, but not as many as some of our fellow diners.

When dinner was over, we caught the last tram down, along with the other happy campers who closed down the place. I was just thinking what a pleasant, innocuous evening it had been when the power failed, leaving us suspended in midair with forty drunken strangers. All of a sudden, the tram car became the setting for something out of a

Fellini movie; people making out, hands everywhere, everyone groping. I was freaking out, but John, who had grown accustomed to that kind of craziness, basically told me to relax, since there was nothing we could do dangling in the middle of the sky.

The following day, Harry kept his doctor's appointment. These photos show us fooling around on the lawn outside the doctor's office building. I guess the groundskeeper felt we were having a little too much fun—he turned the sprinklers on us.

Sarah Kernochan took these three photos. John has my camera lens cover in his mouth.

john & harry

Harry was definitely a free spirit. He and John shared two important bonds: music and the pain of traumatic childhoods. Like John, Harry's father abandoned the family when he was very young, and he'd never gotten over it. Harry liked to party hard, and John was more than happy to join in the revelry. However, Harry could hold his liquor a little better—and wasn't quite as famous as John, who kept making the newspapers.

John had always been a bad drinker from the days in Liverpool. In addition to the outbursts of anger, as John got older alcohol would make him feel physically ill.

Harry and John enjoyed each other's company not so much as close friends than as bad boys. No doubt Harry was an instigator, but John was a willing participant. "C'mon, life's a party," Harry would say. After a couple of months of this party, John straightened up. The toll alcohol had taken on Harry's voice also had a very sobering effect on John. He tried to help Harry, but he was too weak and Harry too strong. Eventually, John quit trying, but expressed his fear that Harry's lifestyle would kill him, which, unfortunately, it ultimately did.

I last saw Harry shortly before he died. We laughed about all our crazy times together, but I noticed a change in him. He had taken John's death very badly and spent the rest of his life crusading for gun control. I didn't see that spark anymore; he seemed to be drifting along, only occasionally making music. Soon after, the party was over.

ellenville, new york, september 1974

My friends Richard and Cynthia Ross owned a restaurant called Home, one of my favorite haunts in the city. I introduced John and Yoko to it, and they became regulars. Richard had a little country cabin in Ellenville, a once-thriving hub in upstate New York (near Woodstock). John had been working nonstop for months (recording *Pussy Cats, Walls and Bridges,* and working with Elton John at Caribou and on Ringo's *Goodnight Vienna* album) and he just wanted to get out of town and relax a bit before tackling *Rock 'n' Roll.* Richard lent us his oasis for a few days.

Just before we went, I attended the first Beatles convention, at John's request, just to see what it was like (and to buy up copies of *Two Virgins* to get them out of circulation). In the dealer room, I passed a table with the most incredibly striking photos of The Beatles, taken in Hamburg in 1961. The man selling the prints, Jürgen Vollmer, was also the photographer. I called John and told him what I had found.

"Jürgen!" he said excitedly. "I haven't seen him in years. Get his number and I want to see those pictures!"

As it happens, Jürgen was living just across the river in Brooklyn. John called him up and invited him over. They were so happy to see each other and spent a wonderful evening reminiscing about the really early days. John got his album cover for *Rock 'n' Roll* that night. Finally, John thought, the pieces of the oldies album were falling into place.

(Left) It was a bright, crisp autumn day and John finally got to wear his Irish knit cable sweater, which he loved. As he hiked up this mountain path with Richard's two dogs, I yelled out to him and, when he turned around, I snapped this photo. John liked it so much he used it for the picture sleeve of the "Imagine" single, which was released in the U.K. on my birthday in 1975.

christmas at
disney world, 1974

S pending Christmas in West Palm Beach was quite surreal—warm and sunny, and
we were hanging out by a pool. Julian loved it. We stayed at Morris Levy's apartment. Morris had a son, Adam, who was close to Julian's age, so they got together a
few times. The *Rock 'n' Roll* album was finally recorded and would be released in March,
1975. We thought the final saga in the most storied of John's albums was behind us; little
did we know the best was yet to come.

Unbeknownst to us, Morris had taken the rough tapes John had given him of the
Rock 'n' Roll sessions and had put together a shoddy mail-order album for his Adam VIII
label (named after his eight-year-old son). In February, ads began appearing on television
for *John Lennon Sings the Great Rock & Roll Hits: Roots*. Besides a horrible, out-of-focus
front cover, the album included songs from the Spector sessions that John hated. All the
tracks were early mixes, which Morris had sped up so they would all fit on the vinyl. John
was forced to rush-release his version, which, due to the time constraints, couldn't be
packaged or promoted as he had planned.

We had no idea this was going on. We were just happy to be in Florida, enjoying another
green Christmas, including a visit to Disney World. Riding the monorail back to our hotel, I
overheard a father tell his son he had heard a Beatle was visiting Disney World. The kid
asked "Which one?" to which the dad replied, "George Harrison." I burst out laughing. John
asked me what I was laughing about and I told him. We all started laughing so loud that
the dad turned to give us a dirty look. At that moment, it registered on the man's face
which Beatle was at the park that day—and that we were laughing at him. "It's O.K., we all
look alike," John joked.

John in the middle of Disney World. Everyone's so intent on getting on the rides that he goes unnoticed.

Julian with Morris Levy and his son, Adam.

The three of us at Morris's apartment. John is wearing the windshield-wiper glasses Julian
bought him for Christmas.

sunset at the
hamptons, new york,
1975

John was beginning to feel like he wanted to "leave the rat race of the city" and get away for a while —but not *too* far away. Since our last break in Ellenville, he'd just come off another whirlwind of work: promoting *Walls and Bridges*, recording *Rock 'n' Roll*, playing live with Elton John, writing and recording "Fame" with David Bowie (which became Bowie's first #1 hit). We were also planning to join Paul and Linda in New Orleans for the recording of their *Venus and Mars* album. John was going to surprise the world (including Paul) by writing and recording with Paul. But he needed a little time to regroup.

We had been frequenting the Hamptons. We found ourselves driving out to Amagansett and popping in on Peter Boyle and his then girlfriend (and eventual wife) Loraine Alterman. Even Allen Klein offered us his place in Westhampton for a week. He had rented a lovely house right on the beach, which couldn't be better for John. We got to know the village grocer and some of the locals in the quaint little community. We also stayed with Mick Jagger out in Montauk in a house he was renting from Andy Warhol. During that visit John and I saw a lovely Scottish-style cottage which was for sale in Montauk, next to the famed lighthouse owned by Peter Beard and overlooking the Atlantic Ocean.

John decided it was time for us to have our own home and asked the real estate agent to show us the place. We fell in love with it and were about to put a binder on it the weekend of February first. Some things just weren't meant to be....

138

acknowledgments

L ife is a journey. I'd like to thank all those who have been a part of mine:

Mal Peachey and John Conway, my book agents at Essential Works in London, who always believed in me and made this book a reality.

Mario Casciano, my right arm throughout this project, who urged me to have these photographs published so the world could see the John he knew and saw during our time together.

Elizabeth Beier, my enthusiastic editor, who showed her love for this book from the very beginning—along with her assistant Michelle Richter (I tried to make it as painless as possible for you), Harriet Seltzer, who always wanted this for St. Martin's, Erin Fiscus for the cover design, Kathryn Parise for the interior design, Courtney Fischer, my publicist, for spreading the word, and the entire St. Martin's team, who spent many hours working on making *Instamatic Karma* a great photo book.

My son Sebastian, for lending his artistic flair on the restoration of my photos—and for trying to keep me calm while I was under deadline.

My daughter Lara, who at sixteen gave me grief, but came through as the primary restorer of my collection through many a long day and night. And it was well worth every bribe she got (especially the PSP).

My mom, Linda Lim Pang, who always stood by me, and to my uncle (Mom's baby brother at age eighty), who has, in the last couple of years, taken care of her so I can work on this book.

"Uncle" Harold Seider, Esq.—without your support and expertise, I would be lost. Your wisdom is immeasurable; your friendship is most cherished. No wonder John loved spending hours in your company.

Cynthia Lennon and Noel Charles...for your friendship and support. We've been through the trenches together and came through the other side with lots of love and happiness all around.

Chip and Beth Pecere of Personal Touch Photography, Inc., for the initial restoration of my photos and for donating their time.

The artist known as Shannon, who came in at the eleventh hour and made sure my photos looked their best.

Friends who shared my time with John:
    Lou Adler, Neil and Susie Aspinall, Spence Berland, Sid Bernstein, Greg Calbi, Candace Carrell, Peppy Castro, Roy Cicala, Al Coury, Ron Delsener, Jack Douglas, Dennis Ferrante, Janice, Troy, and Danielle Germano, Michael Graham, Esq., Bruce Grakal, Peter Jameson, Iris Keitel, Norma Kemper, Sarah Kernochan, Tony King, Allen Klein, David Nutter, Maureen O'Connor, Chris O'Dell, Andrew Loog Oldham, Maria and Armando Ontivero, Richard Perry, Jozy Pollock, Arlene Reckson, Helen and Norman Seaman, Robin Siegel.

Friends—both old and new:
    Billy, Chris and Matty Amendola, Mary Anne and Ames Andersen, Linda Bann, Richard Barone, Mark Bego, Stephanie Bennett, Violet Benny, Jim Bessman, Mitch Borofsky, Shanthi Brigati, Gordon and Vera Brown, Brian Caplan, Esq., Michael and Roberta Cardillo, Rattika and Paul Cartledge, Frank Chmielewski, Jane and Ken Dashow, Juliet and Edward Davies, Andrea Davis, Dwight DeReiter, John Edward, Annie Fowler, Roger Friedman,

Shelley Germeaux, Glauco, Joel Glazier, Fred Goodman, Tyler Elizabeth Graae, Rose Gross-Marino, Leslie and John Hardacre, Susan Hathaway, Sandy Hicks, Denise Jaklitsch, Pat and Tim Jennings, Larry Kane, Mitchell Kanner, Kosh, Beverly Lee, Adrienne and Michael Levin, Louis Levin, Barbara Ligeti, Ken Lubin, Barry Magnus, Tim Mahon, Paul Maiorana, Randi Marcus, Pamela Maythenyi and Don Nissman, Laurie McCaffrey, Mike McCann, Joyce and Sam Moore, Jeannine and Jon Moorehead, Louise deVille Morel, Kathy Morris, "Cousin" Bruce Morrow, Ty Murray, Tony Perkins, Marilyn Petrone, Liliana and Mark Plotkin, Celia Quantrill, Ed and Melani Rogers, Brad Rosenberger, Spencer Ross, Susan Ryan, Greg Schmidt, Pat Sellers, Phoebe Snow, Victor Spinetti, Natasha Stoynoff, Eddie Sung, Peggy Swire, Kate Taylor, Marian Tessa, Rebecca Thornell, Phil Turner, Ellen Voell, Steve Walter, Billy West.

Yoko for giving me—and all of us— "a hole to see the sky through...."

My personal all-star band:

Kenny Ascher, David Brigati, Eddie Brigati, Felix Cavaliere, "Lightning" Lou Christie, Spencer Davis, Gordon Edwards, the Fab Faux, Lawrence Gowan, Justin Hayward, Mick Jagger, Arthur Jenkins, Bobby Keys, Trevor Lawrence, John Lodge, Rick Marotta, Hugh McCracken, The Raspberries, David Spinozza, Mark and Howard of the Turtles, Steven Van Zandt, Jimmy Webb.

Julian for all your help and all the smiles. Your dad would certainly be proud of how his "little man" has become a thoughtful humanitarian and talented artist.

And those who are here in spirit:

Jesse Ed Davis, Mal Evans, Eddie Germano, Michael Hazelwood, Iain Macmillan, Linda McCartney, Keith Moon, Harry Nilsson, Billy Preston, John Ritter, Derek Taylor.

Paul, Ringo, and George for your kindness to me, and for looking after your brother.

And, most important, to John....